TRAVELING WITH OUR STATE

NORTH CAROLINA MOUNTAIN TRAVEL GUIDE

A GUIDE TO YOUR NORTH CAROLINA GETAWAY

What to do, where to eat, and how to make the most of western North Carolina

FROM

Our State
NORTH CAROLINA

GREENSBORO, N.C.

NORTH CAROLINA
MOUNTAIN TRAVEL GUIDE

A GUIDE TO YOUR NORTH CAROLINA GETAWAY

What to do, where to eat, and how to make
the most of a visit to western North Carolina

Published by *Our State* magazine, Greensboro, N.C.

North Carolina Mountain Travel Guide

Published by Mann Media Inc.
P.O. Box 4552, Greensboro, N.C. 27404
(800) 948-1409; ourstate.com
Printed in the United States by R.R. Donnelley

Editor: Elizabeth Hudson
Editorial Designer: Joseph Edwards
Associate Editor: Leah Hughes
Editorial Interns: Ashton Astbury, Julia Sayers
Illustrator: Steven Noble

Library of Congress Control Number:
2012938146

NORTH CAROLINA MOUNTAIN TRAVEL GUIDE

A GUIDE TO YOUR NORTH CAROLINA GETAWAY

TABLE OF CONTENTS

PHOTOGRAPHY BY MATT ROSE

OUTSIDE

PHOTOGRAPHY BY ©ISTOCKPHOTO.COM/DRNADIG

PHOTOGRAPHY BY ROBERT WALTERS

Cherohala Skyway

ONLY 18 MILES OF THE CHEROHALA SKYWAY RUN ACROSS NORTH CAROLINA. BUT THESE MILES ARE SOME OF THE PRETTIEST ANYWHERE.

By Josh Shaffer

PHOTOGRAPHY BY ROBERT WALTERS EMILY CHAPLIN AND CHRIS COUNCIL

Nobody makes cider on the Cherohala Skyway. Nobody serves cheese with a glass of mead. Nobody clogs, plays banjo, makes pottery, blows glass, sells plush bear puppets, or offers any such comfort to a mountain traveler. There's nobody up here. And that's the best part. To hear the bees buzzing in the wildflowers at mile-high Santeetlah overlook, to stand on peaks so high you can almost grab a handful of clouds, to drive two hours through Smoky Mountain country without seeing a single rooftop, you've got to outrun civilization.

This two-lane mountaintop road took roughly 40 years and $100 million to build, a labor-of-Hercules construction job that connects the tiny town of Robbinsville with the tiny town of Tellico Plains, Tennessee. And it runs for only 43 miles, 18 of them in North Carolina.

For most people, just getting to this far-flung stretch requires a daylong drive, the last bit of which means sputtering up hills so steep your car strains in third gear, darting around corners sharp enough to make your steering wheel whinny, and dipping into forests so dark you need headlights at noon. But often, the best places are the hardest to reach. The prettiest views are rewards for the hardest slogs.

Autumn drenches the views along the Cherohala Skyway with color.

To get there

To reach the Cherohala Skyway from Asheville: Follow U.S. Highway 74 West for approximately 70 miles, then turn north onto U.S. Highway 129. Take U.S. Highway 129 to Robbinsville. Merge onto N.C. Highway 143, and drive 12 miles to the beginning of the Cherohala Skyway at Santeetlah Gap.

For more information on the skyway, visit cherohala.org.

For information on accommodations, contact:
Graham County Travel and Tourism
837 Rodney Orr Bypass
Robbinsville, N.C. 28771
(800) 470-3790

You might see a bear. You won't see a gas station.

The famous misty-blue peaks jut out right in front of you, clouds floating like cotton balls at eye level. A sign welcomes you to the Cherohala's official beginning on the North Carolina side: Santeetlah Gap, 2,660 feet.

Some warnings: You might see a bear. You won't see a gas station. You'll need lunch, or at least a snack. If you're lucky, a flying squirrel will come shooting overhead, taking advantage of the artificial tree trunks built as launching pads to aid their flight.

But most important, you won't see many people.

The Cherohala's largest neighbor is Robbinsville, population roughly 700, where the driver's license office is open only on Tuesdays and Phillips Restaurant prides itself on fried green tomatoes. Once you're driving

the Cherohala, you won't hit another inhabited spot until Tellico Plains in Tennessee, which boasts only about 900 residents.

More or less, the last sign of life out of Robbinsville is the hula girl with the swiveling hips on top of the Pineapple Whip stand.

If you do find company here, chances are they'll say the Cherohala scenery equals and sometimes beats the Blue Ridge Parkway. You get more of a sense of being at the top of the mountains rather than in the leafy middles. Vines grow everywhere.

"I'm not saying there's not a better stretch on the Blue Ridge here and there," says David Grimes, a visitor to the skyway from Atlanta, Georgia. "But for 50 miles, it's just a great road. Good pavement. No gravel. All the turns are marked. I'm still waiting for a flying squirrel to come across."

Choices on the Cherohala can be difficult: Slow down to enjoy the view, or speed up to experience the thrill of the curves.

PHOTOGRAPHY BY EMILY CHAPLIN AND CHRIS COUNCIL

PHOTOGRAPHY COURTESY OF THE GRANDFATHER MOUNTAIN STEWARD FOUNDATION

Mile High Swinging Bridge

FOR MORE THAN 50 YEARS, THE BRIDGE HAS CHALLENGED MILLIONS OF VISITORS.

By Leigh Ann Henion

When Hugh Morton inherited Grandfather Mountain in 1952, building the Mile High Swinging Bridge was one of his first orders of business. He was inspired, in part, by his maternal grandmother's limited mobility. He knew that she was no longer able to take rigorous hikes and that she pined for the long-range views she'd enjoyed in her youth.

Morton envisioned a 228-foot suspension bridge to span the 80-foot chasm between Grandfather's Convention Table Rock and Linville Peak. Morton hoped the structure would afford people of all physical abilities the exhilaration of cresting a mountain. When the bridge opened on September 2, 1952, Morton's grandmother, then 90 years old, was once again allowed the high-altitude views she cherished.

Despite its name, the Mile High Swinging Bridge is a relatively solid structure that gives visitors a pathway to Linville Peak.

2

Many visitors don't make it to Linville Peak due to nervousness.

According to Robert Hartley, general manager of Grandfather Mountain from 1968 to 1985 and a lifelong friend of the Morton family, the bridge cost $15,000. The structure was fabricated in Greensboro by the Truitt Manufacturing Company and reassembled on Grandfather Mountain over the course of three weeks by the Craven Steel Erecting Company. Hartley's father, Joseph, oversaw the process. Joseph Hartley advised the Greensboro installation crew to tie the bridge down with cables.

"They made fun of him for that," Hartley recalls. "They said, 'Oh, these old mountain people don't know anything.' But they had never been on Grandfather Mountain in winter when the wind was blowing so hard that you couldn't walk on all fours."

Morton passed away in 2006, but each year, a quarter of a million people visit his mountain and improbable bridge. However, many visitors don't make it to Linville Peak due to nervousness. Years ago, Morton noticed that people were less likely to cross if one or two guests were ahead of them, fearing that their weight would be too much for the structure to bear. So, he put up a sign: "Load Limit 40 Persons." The bridge could actually hold hundreds of people, but visitors seem comfortable when they're able to count 10 or 15 people ahead of them.

The number on the sign may be arbitrary, but it's given many visitors the fortitude to leave solid ground, which isn't actually a mile below the bridge. The name, coined by former North Carolina Tourism Director Charles J. Parker, refers to the bridge's altitude above sea level. The moniker is a bit misleading, but it has an air of drama appropriate for a bridge that moves with the wind as if it's a sailboat on the high seas.

❶ and ❷ Bad weather spawned by a hurricane slowed progress as crews erected the original bridge. ❸ Gov. William Umstead and his daughter, Merle, were the first people to cross the bridge when it opened on September 2, 1952.

Visit

Grandfather Mountain
U.S. Highway 221
Linville, N.C. 28646
(800) 468-7325
grandfathermountain.com

Don't Miss

The Swinging Bridge is completely wheelchair accessible. The Top Shop is equipped with an elevator and an elevated walkway linking the building with the bridge.

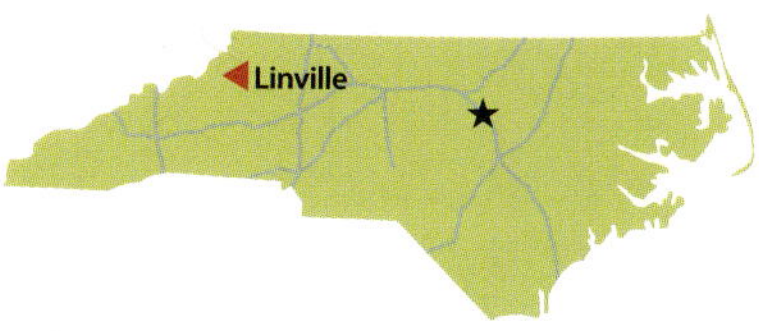

PHOTOGRAPHY BY MIKE BELLEME

Joyce Kilmer Memorial Forest

MORE THAN 3,000 ACRES OF UNCHECKED WILDERNESS AND CENTURIES-OLD TREES.

By Bronwen Dickey

PHOTOGRAPHY BY MIKE BELLEME, EMILY CHAPLIN, AND CHRIS COUNCIL

The two-lane blacktop leading from Robbinsville into the Joyce Kilmer Memorial Forest winds so far into Graham County's green sea of hills that you may be first concerned, and then certain, that you are lost. Fifteen miles doesn't seem like much until you're ascending them in a vertiginous, ever-darkening coil. The farther you go, the denser the canopy becomes, until a woven shroud of poplar, walnut, cherry, and basswood almost closes over the road.

When a forest is left untouched, we can see what grows and moves naturally, like a snail or a birch tree in the Joyce Kilmer Memorial Forest.

To the west lie the dramatic slopes of the Unicoi Range. To the north, the Cheoahs dip and swell. Then the air darkens and cools, whistling along the banks of Little Santeetlah Creek like the forest itself is breathing. And then you aren't lost at all, but wrapped up tight inside something lush and ancient.

The Kilmer is remarkable for one reason: It has been left alone. The axes of logging crews never chewed into these 3,800 acres of Great Smoky Mountains near the Tennessee border. Some sources say the falling prices of timber during the Great Depression saved the forest. Gennett Lumber sold this plot to the federal government in the 1920s, and by 1934, the United

PHOTOGRAPH BY EMILY CHAPLIN & CHRIS COUNCIL

The farther along you head up the two-mile main trail, the darker and greener your field of vision becomes.

States Forest Service had dedicated the untouched vastness to the memory of American poet Joyce Kilmer, author of the famous poem "Trees."

The Kilmer forest is one of the few old-growth forests remaining in the eastern United States. Here, leviathan 400-year-old poplars soar more than 100 feet into the sky, some with circumferences of 20 feet or more, most tucked into lacy banks of Christmas fern and trimmed with trillium and galax and heartleaf.

The farther along you head up the two-mile main trail, the darker and greener your field of vision becomes; step off the trail, and you enter dense, disorienting vegetation, some of the thickest in the Southeast. All secondary trails are only lightly maintained, and signage is pretty much nonexistent. Smart visitors don't venture into the depths of the Kilmer without a good topographic map and a compass. The ones who head in ill-equipped usually wish they hadn't: More hikers have gotten lost in the Joyce Kilmer-Slickrock Wilderness than in any other place in North Carolina.

A combined 18,000 acres is a lot of land to wander.

Ila Hatter uses the majesty of one of the Kilmer's massive poplars to teach her grandson D.J. Gray about nature and the magic it holds.

Visit

Joyce Kilmer Memorial Forest
Topographic maps of the Joyce Kilmer-Slickrock Wilderness, located about 15 miles west of Robbinsville in Graham County, are available at:
Cheoah Ranger District

1070 Massey Branch Road
Robbinsville, N.C. 28711
For more information, contact the ranger office at (828) 479-6431.

Don't Miss

Cherokee legends frequently include the yumwi, or little people, who inhabit the oldest trees. Like elves or gnomes in European fairy tales, the yumwi are said to exercise mischief on just about everyone, except the very young and the very old, whom they protect and care for.

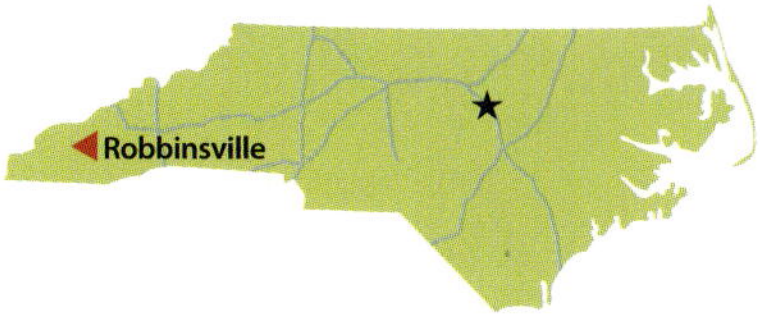

Camp Raven Knob

A RESERVATION IN SURRY COUNTY GIVES BOY SCOUTS THE TIME AND SPACE TO LEARN LIFE'S LESSONS.

By Chip Womick

PHOTOGRAPHY BY DANA MACKAY

From the ground, some 500 feet beneath it, the knob is not all that impressive. But put on your walking shoes and start climbing toward the sky.

The path up follows a series of switchbacks, snaking ever closer to Raven Knob. It's a 40-minute hike, give or take a few minutes, depending on your stamina and determination.

Once you're standing on the knob, a panorama unfolds and the gray outcropping takes on a new meaning. Look north, and you can see the mountains of Virginia in the distance. Look down, and Camp Raven Knob spreads out like a miniature playland for energetic youth, with a collection of campsites and trails, a climbing tower and a ropes course, and a pristine, private lake for swimming and boating. Use a little imagination, and the outline of that lake, Lake Sabotta, resembles a raven.

Camp Raven Knob — officially Raven Knob Scout Reservation — stands on 3,200 acres of unspoiled land in Surry County.

For more than half a century, Boy Scouts have made memories that last a lifetime at Camp Raven Knob, which has 35 different campsites.

An amphitheater that seats 2,000 overlooks Lake Sabotta.

Arvil Sale of Boone is the camp handicrafts director, a position he's had for 30 years.

"Raven Knob is a unique place, kind of a sanctuary for those of us who enjoy getting a little bit back to nature and having a respite from the everyday life that we live."

Scouts can choose from 100 activity sessions on any given day, everything from rifle and archery to photography and personal fitness. And, of course, there's always the camp classic: canoeing.

If you're going

Raven Knob Scout Reservation
266 Raven Knob Road
Mount Airy, N.C. 27030
(336) 352-4307

Don't Miss

The Zeb Barnhardt Training Center is a perfect retreat site for Scouters, church groups, and small companies.

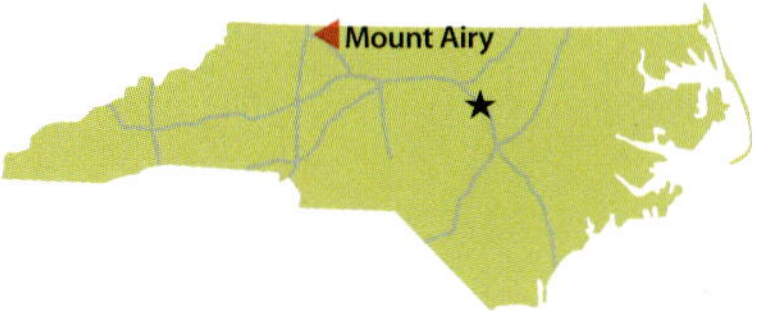

The Appalachian Trail

YOU HAVE TO WORK TO SAVOR THE MAJESTY OF THE APPALACHIAN TRAIL, BUT THERE'S MUCH TO APPRECIATE — AND PRESERVE.

By John Manuel

PHOTOGRAPHY BY MATT ROSE

The Appalachian Trail is not your usual natural attraction. For one, it is more than 2,000 miles long, crossing 14 states from Maine to Georgia. The North Carolina portion is nearly 300 miles long, strung across some of the most inaccessible countryside in the state.

In North Carolina, most of the AT passes through the Great Smoky Mountains National Park, and the Pisgah and Nantahala National Forests. So it is protected for some distance on both sides. However, in some places, the corridor is only as wide as the footpath itself, and the trail is exposed to activities like logging, mining, road building, and development.

Balds are one of the natural wonders of the southern Appalachians. Most of the range's peaks are covered in trees, but some are open, carpeted in grass or shrubs. No one is sure what caused

The Appalachian Trail crosses the Roan Highlands, and the views atop Roan Bluff at the end of Cloudland Trail go on forever.

PHOTOGRAPHY BY MATT ROSE

1

2

No one is sure what caused these balds — fire, grazing cattle, or prehistoric grazers like the woolly mammoth.

these openings — fire, farmers grazing their cattle, or prehistoric grazers like the woolly mammoth. Hikers love them because they afford 360-degree views. Botanists value them for their ecology.

❶ With its view of the Roaring Creek Valley, the Overmountain Shelter is a favorite stop for hikers. ❷ The Cloudland Trail leads hikers through stands of rhododendrons. ❸ The Appalachian Trail runs across the top of Big Bald, which feels like it's on top of the world.

From the Overmountain Shelter on the far side of Big Yellow Mountain, you can hike over Grassy Ridge, Jane Bald, and Round Bald headed for Roan High Bluff, elevation 5,800 feet. Cross N.C. Highway 261 at Carver's Gap and begin your climb through the magical world of the spruce-fir forest. On most of the high-elevation peaks, the spruce-fir forests are dying, victims of an insect called the woolly adelgid. But here on the Roan, they thrive.

If you're going

Hikers in search of a break on North Carolina's 88 miles of trail may wish to stop in Hot Springs (the trail runs right down the main street).

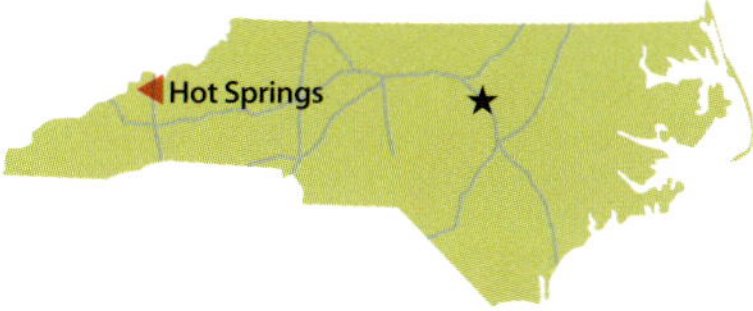

PHOTOGRAPHY BY ©ISTOCKPHOTO.COM/ARTIST'SMARCELODUFFLOCOW

Fishing Western Waters

WHERE WELL-STOCKED WATERS AND GORGEOUS SETTINGS MAKE THE PERFECT DAY.

By Troy Baker

Thousands of miles of trout-filled rivers, streams, and creeks flow across North Carolina's western counties. Many are stocked by the North Carolina Wildlife Resources Commission (NCWRC), almost guaranteeing success every time you wade into the water. Others are more remote and challenge even the experienced fisher to snare the wily wild trout.

Some streams, however, are more productive than others. Here, we offer our seven favorites:

1 **Davidson River, Transylvania County** Designated by NCWRC as Catch & Release Fly-Fish Only, the river's headwaters contain some of the largest trout in North Carolina and have more brown, rainbow, and brook trout per mile than any other stream in the state.

Access: U.S. Highway 64, near Brevard.

Spend some time in the creeks and rivers of western North Carolina, where a great catch of brown trout is just about guaranteed.

2 Nantahala River, Macon County

The Nantahala starts out as a small headwater that opens up into a large river. The Nantahala has a delayed harvest section, which means that NCWRC stocks it the first week of the months of October, November, March, April, and May. Wild native trout also populate this river. A dam regulates the river's flow, so keep watch for rising water.

Access: U.S. Highway 74 and Wayah Road, near Rainbow Springs.

3 Tuckasegee River, Jackson County

The Tuckasegee runs through several small towns, including Dillsboro, Cullowhee, East Laport, and Tuckasegee. For this reason, it has several access points. The river also tends to have larger trout. Like the Nantahala, the delayed harvest section of the river experiences water level changes.

Access: U.S. Highway 74 and N.C. Highway 107

4 Wilson Creek, Caldwell County

Wilson Creek stretches up the backside of Grandfather Mountain and tumbles down into a valley where it joins the John River in Caldwell County. There's a delayed harvest section on the river, creating a beautiful spot for fly-fishing. A welcome center located near this section of the river makes it one of the easiest waterways to access. An unpaved road also runs the length of the river.

Access:
Wilson Creek Visitor Center
7805 Brown Mountain Beach Road
Collettsville, N.C. 28611

5 Watauga River, Watauga County

One of the easiest places to access this trout stream is in Valle Crucis. It offers several sections for fishing and flows through a park with a playground and walking trails. Here, you'll find brown and rainbow trout and an occasional brook trout. When you're ready for a lunch break, you don't even have to shed your waders before heading over to Mast General Store for a meal and drink.

Access: N.C. Highway 194 in Valle Crucis.

6 East Prong Roaring River, Wilkes County

For easy access, you can't beat the East Prong Roaring River at Stone Mountain State Park; the river also offers handicap access. The river has a delayed harvest section and other small streams that are designated as wild streams. Brown, rainbow, and brook trout swim this river and make for easy fishing.

Access:
Stone Mountain State Park
3042 Frank Parkway
Roaring Gap, N.C. 28668

7 Helton Creek, Ashe County

Helton Creek flows among rolling hills and lush, green meadows, a perfect setting for fishing the delayed harvest waters. The road

Even the lures used for fly-fishing project beauty and serenity.

follows the stream, providing access almost anywhere on the river. The stream is stocked with all three species of trout, while lunkers also consider flies tossed their way.
Access: N.C. Highway 16 just north of the New River.

Go Fish

North Carolina Wildlife Resources Commission
(919) 707-0010
ncwildlife.org/fishing

NCWRC provides information on designated trout waters, including locations, regulations, and maps. The commission is also a good source of general information on fishing in North Carolina.

Davidson River Outfitters
95 Pisgah Highway
Pisgah Forest, N.C. 28768
(888) 861-0111
davidsonflyfishing.com

Curtis Wright Outfitters
24 North Main Street
Weaverville, N.C. 28787
(828) 645-8700
curtiswrightoutfitters.com

Mac Brown, Guide
McLeod's Highland Fly-Fishing
779 West Deep Creek
Bryson City, N.C. 28713
(828) 488-8975
macbrownflyfish.com

BILTMORE

PHOTOGRAPHY BY STACEY VAN BERKEL

Biltmore Insider's Tour

FOUR BEHIND-THE-SCENES TOURS OF THE STATE'S GRANDEST HOME.

By Leigh Ann Henion

PHOTOGRAPHY BY STACEY VAN BERKEL

1 The Butler's Tour

It's hard to believe that the Biltmore House was a bachelor pad, complete with a billiards room and a bowling alley. In total, there are 250 rooms in the house. That includes 35 guest and family rooms, 43 bathrooms, and three kitchens. George remained single for the first three years he lived there, until he married Edith Stuyvesant Dresser.

Chuck Holmes, a Biltmore guide, often begins his specialty Butler's Tour in the bachelors' staircase, which houses curiosities including a mounted caribou with a third antler growing out of its forehead. Holmes then moves toward the boiler room. The subbasement's acreage is dedicated to the inner workings of the house, and some of the most impressive hardware in the place is located in the dynamo room. The Biltmore House had electricity from 1895 onward.

Holmes walks through the water-supply room, past a Tabasco water heater, and into the refrigeration room, which once housed an innovative ammonia-gas-and-brine system that made ice cubes at a time when iced tea in summer would have been a miraculous treat.

The Architect's Tour takes visitors to the rooftop for amazing views and a closer look at artful stonework.

2 The Vanderbilt Family and Friends Tour

On the Biltmore's Vanderbilt Family and Friends Tour, Biltmore guide Sharon Brookshire explains that the rooms on this tour were arbitrarily assigned to historic guests so curators can give present-day visitors a better understanding of how the house functioned during George and Edith's lifetime.

Room after room, she shares stories

of the Vanderbilts' loved ones. They came to Asheville to evade kidnappers, to mourn the loss of family members, to create art, to recuperate from illnesses.

The individuals who catered to the Vanderbilts' guests were also provided storybook nooks to call their own. Brookshire enters a narrow hallway of unadorned plaster on a servants' floor for single females. Each bedroom is outfitted with a rocking chair and a tiny window, a porthole to view the earthen sea beyond.

3 Legacy of the Land Tour

Dave Richard, a retired schoolteacher, leads Biltmore's Legacy of the Land Tour, a driving tour of the grounds. On the trip, he shows people the black-and-white images of what the estate looked like when George first bought it.

The approach road, the final stretch of Richard's tour, is currently undergoing a 10-year restoration. The road's gentle curves lead into a fantasyland, following a path that burrows into nature.

The surrounding forest — composed of azalea, mountain laurel, dogwood, redwood, and oak trees — appears as wilderness, but it's actually a strategically designed woodland garden.

4 The Architect's Tour

Jane Hunnicutt, a veteran Biltmore guide, pauses at the top of the house's grand staircase — an impressive limestone spiral of 102 steps — and gestures toward the ornate cast-iron railing. "If you're not afraid of

Just as George Vanderbilt planned it, Biltmore House emerged as a fantastical vision as guests rounded the last curve of the approach road and their gaze fell upon the mansion.

1

2

3

4

5

Most items in the Biltmore House come with a story. 1 The Biltmore's boiler hints at the estate's high-tech opulence. 2 Edith's trunks tell of a life of travel. 3 The organ, although 100 years old, didn't arrive at Biltmore until 1999. 4 The caribou was just one of the animal heads George Vanderbilt ordered out of a catalog. 5 The gold shoes are a re-creation of what the Vanderbilt family and friends may have worn.

heights," she says, "this is a great staircase to look down."

She's used to people getting nervous on her tours. After all, the Architect's Tour, which includes a visit to the Biltmore roof, isn't for the faint of heart.

Hunnicutt leads the group through the observatory, to the vestibule balcony. The balcony is narrow, so much so that some visitors are forced to move along the roofline with their backs against the exterior wall. The view is worth it.

The Architect's Tour — once known as the Rooftop Tour — often ends on the west balcony, which looks over one of the most spectacular backyards in the world.

❶ George and Edith's engagement photos, circa 1898, are on display in the Morland room, creating a sense that the family has only stepped away. ❷ and ❸ The clothes on display in the rooms are re-creations of what the family and guests may have worn. Their actual clothes aren't available. ❹ What Biltmore's subbasement lacked in beauty it made up for in technology, including a water heater and an ice maker.

Visit

Biltmore Estate
1 Lodge Street
Asheville, N.C. 28803
(800) 411-3812
biltmore.com

Don't Miss

After the grand house tour, stop by the winery, and enjoy a tasting of Biltmore's award-winning reds and whites. A guided visit of the winery and complimentary tasting is included in estate admission.

GARDENS

PHOTOGRAPHY BY ©ISTOCKPHOTO.COM/MONIA33

Wildcat Ridge Farm

WHEN A COUPLE IN CLYDE NEEDED SOMETHING TO CARRY THEM INTO THEIR NEXT STAGE OF LIFE, THE PEONY BECAME THEIR SAVING GRACE.

By Jason Smith

PHOTOGRAPHY BY EMILY CHAPLIN AND CHRIS COUNCIL

If you want to walk through rows and rows of blooms the size of dinner plates — through a thousand bursts of pink and fuchsia and buttermilk and tissue-paper white nodding agreeably in the mountain breeze and calling you sweetly with scents that make you swoon — if you want to take all of that in and maybe take some of it home with you, you have three weeks, and only three weeks. Go and find your calendar and write it down: the last week of April, give or take, and the first few weeks of May.

That's when the peonies bloom at Wildcat Ridge Farm in Clyde. And that's when you can make an appointment to walk the rows with Ricardo and Suzanne Fernandez, who own the place. Up here, peony season is short and sweet. You choose the blooms you want; Ricardo and Suzanne will cut. You can buy potted peonies, too. People come from as far away as Raleigh and Atlanta, Georgia.

The 'Cora Louise' is an intersectional peony that can produce up to 50 blooms in a season.

In 2004, Ricardo and Suzanne weren't growing peonies. They ran their own restaurant, planning for outdoor cooking classes at a giant, brick grill Ricardo built on the bank of the Pigeon River beside their house. They tended to a 30-by-100-foot greenhouse full of prize-winning orchids.

Then, Hurricane Frances hit. It rained all day and night, and the Pigeon River brushed the couple's doorstep. Then, Hurricane Ivan came, and it was

worse. "Everything was knocked down, sent down the river, or washed onto our property from upstream," Suzanne says. "All our raised garden beds for the restaurant — gone. There was nothing left."

"Not one orchid," Ricardo says. "So we needed to start again."

They couldn't do orchids again. "It was just too painful," Suzanne says. So they hit upon peonies.

"The thing that I love about the peonies," Suzanne says, "is that … well, I believe you should eat according to the seasons. And I believe that you should enjoy things according to their season. So if a peony just blooms for three weeks once a year, I think that's great. That's OK. You know? That's life."

❶ Suzanne and Ricardo Fernandez are from opposite ends of the globe, but for the past 34 years, they've been through everything together, leading them to a field of peonies. ❷ The 'Bartzella' was the American Peony Society's 2007 Peony of the Year. ❸ Wildcat Ridge Farm in Clyde draws people from all over the state during the short peony season. ❹ The 'Gay Paree' is an herbaceous peony, which means it dies back to the root every fall.

Visit

3553 Panther Creek Road
Clyde, N.C. 28721
(828) 627-6751
wildcatridgefarm.com

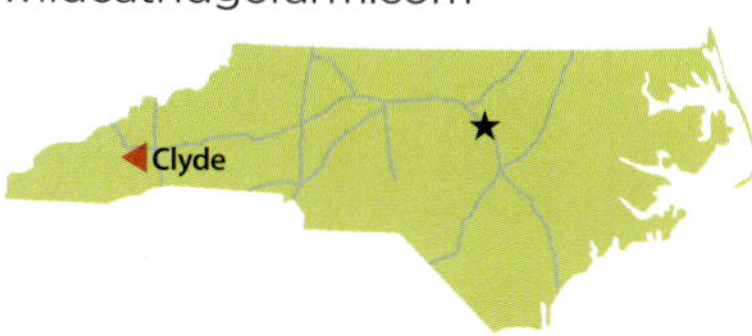

SINCE
1891
Gardens of the Blue Ridge

Gardens of the Blue Ridge

AT THE OLDEST LICENSED NURSERY IN THE STATE, NATIVE SPECIES CARRY ON THE LEGACY OF THIS LAND.

By Leigh Ann Henion

PHOTOGRAPHY BY CHERYL ZIBISKY

Most of the time, dead plants fill the Gardens of the Blue Ridge greenhouses. At least, that's what a lot of visitors think.

"You go into a regular garden center, and everything's in bloom," says Rob Fletcher. "But with native plants, you'd have to come every two to three weeks to catch something flowering."

Gardens of the Blue Ridge is the oldest licensed nursery in North Carolina. At least one member of Rob's family has operated the Newland business since 1892. Rob and his parents now handle daily operations, with the help of other family during the busy seasons in spring and winter.

The nursery specializes in wildflowers and shade plants that thrive in the temperate rain forests of southern Appalachia.

The majority of the nursery's business is mail-order, but it has quite a few local customers. Over the years, Rob developed an honor system that allows people to take what they want after hours, leaving payment in a mailbox. "We think people who like wildflowers tend to be good people," Rob says.

When the sign company sent the Gardens of the Blue Ridge sign with the incorrect date, 1891 instead of 1892, the Fletcher family put it up anyway. What's one year when you've been in business for more than a century?

Visit

Gardens of the Blue Ridge
9056 Pittmans Gap Road
Newland, N.C. 28657
(828) 733-2417
gardensoftheblueridge.com
Hours vary depending on the season.

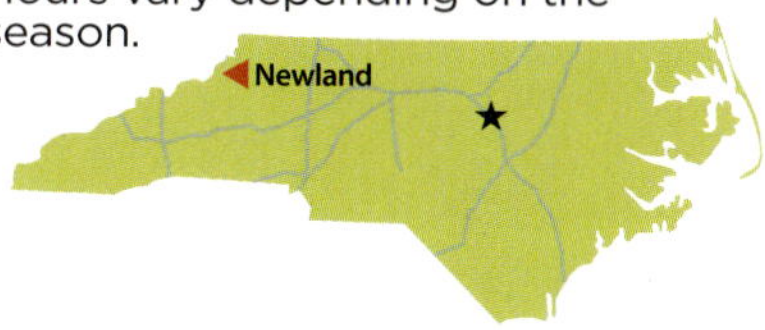

N.C. Arboretum

A CENTURY AGO, AMERICA'S PREMIER LANDSCAPE ARCHITECT DESIGNED THE STATE'S FIRST ARBORETUM.

By Sarah Perry

PHOTOGRAPHY BY EMILY CHAPLIN AND CHRIS COUNCIL

From the time man has lived on Earth, he's shared it with nature.

Somewhere along the way, we decided we should have a say in things. We should be able to contain flowers in pots, place the dogwood in that one position where the evening light hits it just so.

Sometimes it works.

Sometimes it doesn't.

At the North Carolina Arboretum in Asheville, the staff members are experts in maintaining that balance — they've got it down to a science. They know when to let things grow wild and free, and when to prune and perfect in such a way that shows the best side of that plant or tree. They use mathematics and the same software architects use to design plant spaces. Clara Curtis, the director for design and exhibit assets, knows it takes 3,456 violas or pansies to complete her quilt-garden design.

There are 24 blocks in the quilt garden. Each block represents a square in a quilt. Over the years, the blocks have been pieces of a log cabin, a flower basket, a double wedding ring.

Grapevines thread their way along the teaching shelter, and coneflowers and honeysuckle line the perimeter.

Curtis designs the garden nearly a year in advance. She chooses a pattern, something to represent the mountains. She fills in the blank pattern, rotating and turning the blocks until they lock together in a kaleidoscope of colors. She never wants more than five divisions of space in each block — that can be too much. Too busy. In each space, she can use five kinds of plants.

After she finishes designing, she meets with the gardeners and landscape supervisors. She needs them to grow her plants in specific pots — sometimes four-inch-deep pots, sometimes five-inch, sometimes in flats. She needs 3,456 plants each spring, maybe a few extra, for the 1,536-square-foot garden.

When you walk the grounds of the arboretum, you can see Curtis's influence there. When the fog lifts in the morning in the heritage garden, you find yourself wrapped in a dewy emerald grove. You see the grapevines creeping up the wooden teaching shelter, teardrops of water sliding from the leaves of honeysuckle and marigolds, and you inhale the scent of rich humus soil and spring rain. Walk past the grove of American holly trees;

1

2

The plan for the North Carolina Arboretum began nearly two centuries ago.

touch their rubbery, spiky leaves; and enter the plants of promise garden where you see a tree with cinnamon-colored bark that peels in layers — a magnificent paperbark maple.

The plan for the North Carolina Arboretum began nearly two centuries ago. George Vanderbilt chose the nation's renowned landscape architect, Frederick Law Olmsted, to design the grounds for his Biltmore Estate. Olmsted grew famous after he created New York's Central Park. Olmsted was a visionary. When he saw the ragged forests, he formed a plan. He wanted an arboretum, a "tree museum," as he called it, where he could grow dozens of species of trees.

But he couldn't convince Vanderbilt that an arboretum was right for his estate. Vanderbilt wanted a park. Olmsted wanted a museum. They settled on restoring the forests and setting aside some land for gardens.

Olmsted was in his 70s when he took on the project. He was always an insomniac, but when his plans for the arboretum fell through, he slept even less. In the summer of 1895, his mind grew so weak, he wrote the same letter to Biltmore three times. In letter after letter, he wrote that Biltmore and his staff simply didn't understand the importance of an arboretum. He died in 1903 at age 81. Nearly 100 years later, plans for his arboretum finally took hold.

In 1986, the state of North Carolina and the United States Forest Service struck an agreement. The state could use 426 acres of land in the Pisgah National Forest to build an arboretum. The General Assembly set aside $250,000 for the arboretum's first year. The next year, workers planted the first tree on the property — a monarch birch — on Arbor Day.

By 1990, the staff grew to 24 employees, and workers erected and built the education center.

In 1998, a crowd gathered beside the education center, at the top of the winding, one-mile stretch of road. The director, standing next to Olmsted's descendants, announced the dedication.

Nearly 100 years after Olmsted died, the board named its road after him.

The arboretum's address: 100 Frederick Law Olmsted Way.

❶ The stream garden was designed to capture the sound of water flowing over rocks, just like a mountain creek. ❷ The gardens at the arboretum boast hundreds of plants, including this coneflower.

Visit

The North Carolina Arboretum
100 Frederick Law Olmsted Way
Asheville, N.C. 28806
ncarboretum.org

Burgers BBQ & Breakfast

PHOTOGRAPHY BY MATT HULSMAN

Jimmy Mac's

A MENU WITH 20 DIFFERENT BURGERS IS REASON ENOUGH TO STOP BY THE POPULAR BRYSON CITY RESTAURANT.

By David Bailey

PHOTOGRAPHY BY MATT ROSE

When you drop by Jimmy Mac's in downtown Bryson City, don't be surprised if your greeter is two and a half feet tall and 3 years old. "Come with me," Katelyn McNorrill says, handing customers a menu and flashing a grin.

"She's the third generation," says James McNorrill III — Little Jimmy to most people. Jimmy Mac's Restaurant is famous in these parts for its list of 20 burgers.

Located in what was once the old post office, Jimmy Mac's continues a family tradition of serving award-winning burgers.

Eat one of Jimmy Mac's creations, and you're not inclined to argue. The two-fisted, juicy gourmet burgers are some of the best on the planet. Take the Bleu Max — a softball-size burger, seared to medium-rare juiciness, sandwiched on a fresh-baked bun; it's got enough bleu cheese and bacon on it to make a second sandwich.

Whether it's the Minnesota Fats with mushroom gravy, sour cream, and sauteed onions or the Cheese, Cheese, Cheese Burger with mozzarella, cheddar, and swiss, Jimmy Mac's burgers are not for the timid but promise satisfaction across a spectrum of tastes. And beef patties aren't the only option — all 20 variations can dress up buffalo burgers, elk burgers, and even veggie burgers.

Jimmy Mac's opened in July 2006, and it's been a family enterprise ever since.

For Little Jimmy and Kim McNorrill and even their daughter, Katelyn, serving up gourmet burgers, such as the Cajun burger, is all in the family.

Eat

Jimmy Mac's Restaurant
121 Main Street
Bryson City, N.C. 28713
(828) 488-4700
Hours: Sunday, Monday, Wednesday, and Thursday, 11:15 a.m.-8:30 p.m.; Friday and Saturday, 11:15 a.m.-9:30 p.m.

Don't Miss

If you've still got an appetite for adventure after downing one of the big burgers at Jimmy Mac's, take a tour of western North Carolina's tree canopy with a zip line ride. For reservations, Nantahala Gorge Canopy Tours, (828) 488-2384 or wildwaterrafting.com/nantahala.php.

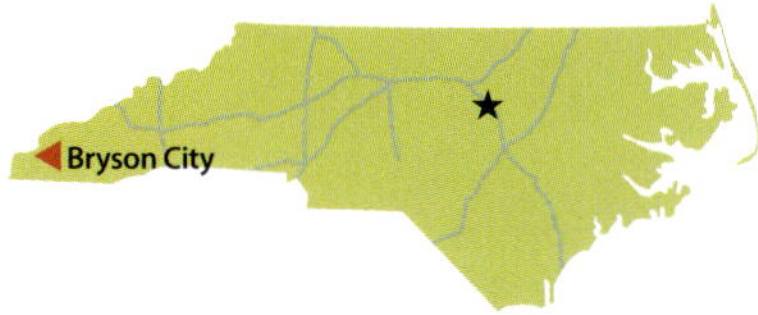

Luella's Bar-B-Que

CUSTOMERS FIND ENOUGH FAMILIARITY TO MAKE THEM COMFORTABLE AND ENOUGH DIVERSITY TO REMIND THEM THEY'RE IN ASHEVILLE.

By Leah Hughes

PHOTOGRAPHY BY MATT ROSE

When Jeff Miller opened Luella's Bar-B-Que four years ago, he created a restaurant with a strong sense of place and a deep understanding of its customers. Located just north of downtown Asheville, Luella's attracts a varied crowd.

Luella's top seller is still the pork barbecue sandwich with slaw and a side of macaroni and cheese.

"We wanted to put a new line around barbecue," Miller says. He doesn't know exactly how to define it. Maybe it's the decor. Maybe it's the five different sauces. Maybe it's the brisket, turkey, and chicken in addition to the pork.

But whatever it is, it's authentic. Miller opened Luella's in 2007, named after his grandmother and his 6-year-old daughter, who loves the macaroni and cheese.

Two years ago, Miller relocated Luella's from south Asheville to the current building, which once housed Boston Pizza, a neighborhood gathering place and popular hangout for students.

He added an item to the menu called Big Boy's Blue Ribbon BBQ Platter. The platter — served on old pizza pans he found in the attic of the restaurant — includes a half-pound each of pork barbecue, pulled chicken, and sliced beef brisket, and eight ribs. With your choice of three sides and a dozen hush puppies.

Maybe Miller doesn't know how to define Luella's, but that one platter does a pretty good job.

Customers at Luella's can try something different or stick to the North Carolina standard: a chopped-pork sandwich.

Eat

Luella's Bar-B-Que
501 Merrimon Avenue
Asheville, N.C. 28804
(828) 505-7427
luellasbbq.com

Don't Miss

Luella's offers live music during Sunday brunch from noon-2 p.m.

1

2

3

Joey's Pancake House

ANYONE WHO HAS EATEN BREAKFAST AT JOEY'S KNOWS THE FOOD IS DELICIOUS AND THE SERVICE IS EXCEPTIONAL.

By Tommy Tomlinson

PHOTOGRAPHY BY JESSI BLAKELY

It's Saturday morning at Brenda O'Keefe's restaurant — Joey's Pancake House in Maggie Valley — and she's at a lectern in the center aisle, steering the action like a ship captain at the wheel. She's been running this place for 44 years, and for much of that time, it's been one of the most popular breakfast places in the state. On a busy day, like this one, Joey's serves 700 to 800 customers. And it's only open from 7 a.m. until noon.

Brenda met her husband, Joe O'Keefe, in Miami Beach, where they worked at the famous Fontainebleau Hotel. They came to Maggie Valley to visit friends in the summer of 1966. As they lingered in town, they noticed a little restaurant building that was up for lease.

"My mother and sister had been in the restaurant business, so I knew a little about it," she says. "Joey had never been out of a silk suit. He had never cooked an egg in his life."

But when you are newly in love, there are no obstacles, only adventures. They went back to Miami Beach, packed up their stuff, and came back to the mountains. They opened the little restaurant and named it Joey's — down in Miami Beach, he had gone by Joe, but they decided Joey sounded friendlier. They learned to cook eggs and went home every night with pancake mix on their shoes.

For years, they stayed open from 7 a.m. to 3 p.m., but then Joey had what Brenda calls a "heart incident," and they cut back the hours. Joey loved being at the restaurant, though. He moved out to the cash register and chatted with all the customers he had waved at from the kitchen all those years. He kept working until his heart gave out. That was November 29, 2001. He was 83.

People asked, reasonably, if she was

❶ The silver dollar pancakes at ❷Joey's are so good, folks line up for them. ❸Brenda O'Keefe believes in good food, a clean restaurant, and stellar service.

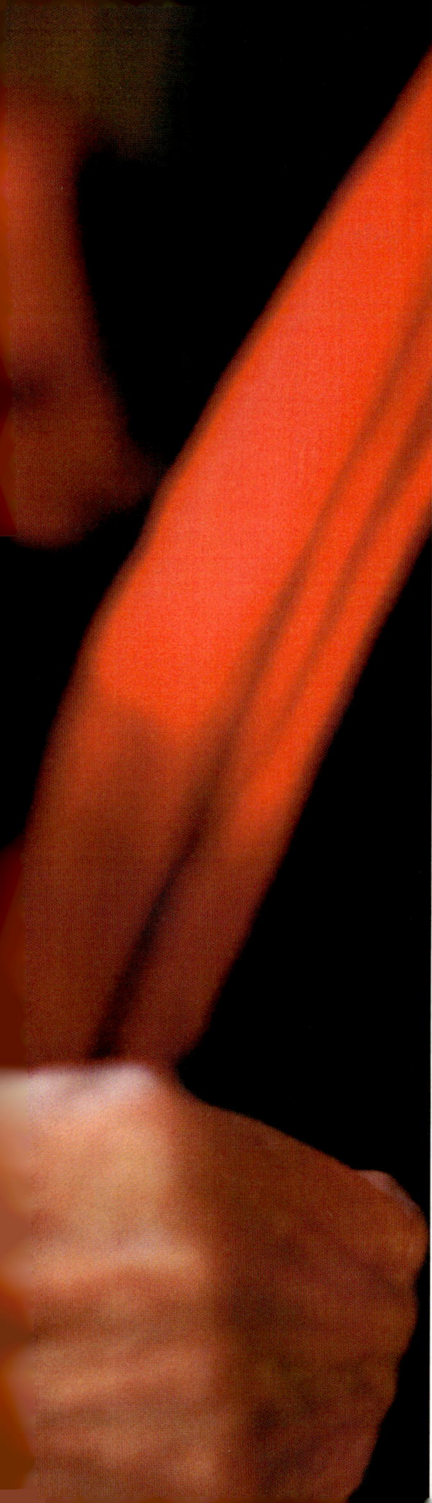

Mounds of blueberries and whipped cream move the waffles at Joey's Pancake House beyond beautiful.

going to close the restaurant. But she had 55 people working for her. And she knew Joey would want her to stay.

It is a business, but Brenda thinks of it as a family, too, and of course you know who is first in her heart. Joey's name is still on the sign, and his face is still on the menu, and Brenda says she can feel him in the building. She never expected to be here, never expected to be doing this. But it's been 44 years now, and she's proud of what she and Joey built.

Eat

Joey's Pancake House
4309 Soco Road (U.S. Highway 19)
Maggie Valley, N.C. 28751
(828) 926-0212
joeyspancake.com

April-October, open daily, 7 a.m.-noon (except Thursdays); November-February, open Friday-Monday, 7 a.m.-noon; Closed during March.

Don't Miss

After breakfast, stop in at Wheels Through Time, an all-American motorcycle museum displaying more than 300 classic Harleys, Indians, Excelsiors, and Hendersons. (828) 926-6266 or wheelsthroughtime.com.

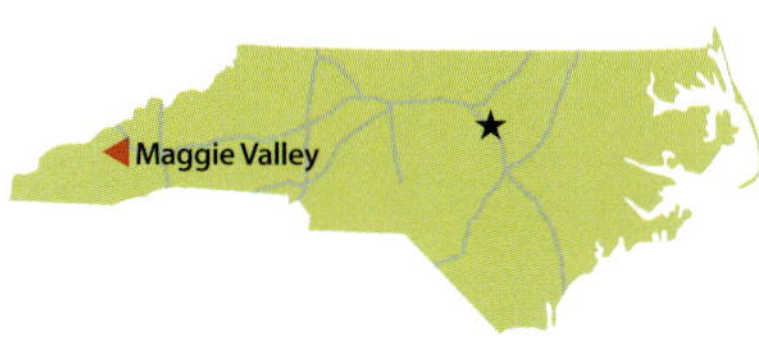

PHOTOGRAPHY BY MATT ROSE

Breakfast in the West

WHEN YOU GET BACK UP IN THE HILLS, BREAKFAST IS OFTEN ABOUT THE SLOWER PACE OF LIFE.

By David Bailey
PHOTOGRAPHY BY MATT ROSE

Glen Alpine Depot
102 Linville Street,
Glen Alpine (828) 584-0202

Don't miss the hash browns and biscuits with butter and blackberry jam

Saturday mornings are Depot mornings, says Emily Alexander. "If we are in town, we are there." She and her husband, David, go to the Depot for the food, served up by owner Mary Haller. "I always have the same thing every week: fluffy scrambled eggs, hash browns, sausage, and a scrumptious biscuit with butter and blackberry jam. Mary's hash browns are the best, a perfect mix of crunchiness and tender."

But the real difference comes from Mary and her staff.

"The Depot is our special place. There are so many regulars there each weekend that it's like seeing family. … It's the one time in the week we can eat breakfast and linger over coffee and just talk — no rush, no deadlines."

Scrumptious biscuits and sausage entice customers to linger at the Glen Alpine Depot.

Onions
Buttered, Spiced

Peter's Pancakes & Waffles
1384 Tsali Boulevard,
Cherokee
(828) 497-5116

Don't miss the Huevos Enrique, a loaded omelet

Michele Galloway and her husband, Dale, both teach in Cherokee and both love breakfast food. "Breakfast reminds me of weekends spent with my grandparents when I would wake up smelling biscuits, gravy, bacon, and eggs," she says.

When Galloway wants to revive those memories, she heads to Peter's Pancakes, a small, family-owned restaurant on the Oconaluftee River. Galloway is partial to the pancakes, which "are light in texture and have a wonderful, homemade taste. They will make them anyway you want them — with blueberries or pecans, a short stack or tall, or even multigrain."

Her 13-year-old son, Aidan, orders Huevos Enrique (Eric's Eggs). The dish, created by the restaurant's operator, Eric Hooper, is a large omelet with sauteed potatoes and onions, sweet peppers, bacon, cheese, salsa, sour cream, and jalapeños on the side.

Dan'l Boone Inn
130 Hardin Street, Boone
(828) 264-8657

Don't miss the homemade black cherry preserves

When we asked readers to tell us about their favorite North Carolina breakfast spots, there was one standout among the 254 responses — the Dan'l Boone Inn. Many of those responses came from readers who echoed the comments of Rhyne Garris: "Man, do they ever bring you some food. If you're looking for a fruit-and-yogurt plate, this may not be the place to come."

For anyone who hasn't bellied up to the inn's family-style, all-you-can-eat country breakfast, Garris, who lives on Beech Mountain, fills you in on exactly what you can expect. "They come pushing a cart loaded down with steaming bowls of scrambled eggs, grits, country apples, sausage gravy, hot biscuits and jelly, toast, platters of country ham, sausage, bacon, and more country ham with redeye gravy," he says.

The inn's country ham, locally cured by Watauga farmers, is a can't-miss. And make sure you get some of the homemade black cherry preserves. "My dad absolutely has to purchase a pint or two of black cherry preserves to take back home to Onslow County to share with his breakfast buddies," Garris says.

Now that Garris's twin sons are seniors at Appalachian State University, the extended Garris family meets at the restaurant often for special gatherings. "When we get together for a good breakfast, it takes us back to a simpler time," Garris says, "and the conversation takes us to loved ones who are no longer with us."

A Peter's Pancakes & Waffles original, the Huevos Enrique satisfies the heartiest of appetites.

1

Ward's Dairy Bar & Grill
24 Main Street, Saluda
(828) 749-2321

Don't miss Charlie Ward's homemade sausage

"Under old management" is not a marketing strategy likely to blaze any new trails, but it sure works for Judy Ward, who reopened Ward's Dairy Bar & Grill in Saluda on July 9, 2010, at 6 a.m. sharp — to a capacity crowd.

The popular grill and landmark in downtown Saluda started when Judy's in-laws opened it in 1939. Judy's husband, Charlie Ward, worked behind the counter as a boy and eventually, with Judy's help, took over management of the popular diner. The couple retired in 2007 and sold the restaurant, so they could take it easy for a change.

Charlie Ward passed away about a year after they sold the grill.

After Charlie died, Judy called a relative, Clark Thompson, who for the last 38 years has specialized in restoring old buildings in Pensacola, Florida. The two of them reopened the grill, with Thompson leading the total renovation of the diner and the adjoining Thompson Store. Charlie Ward's legendary homemade sausage, made from Boston butts, is still on the menu, along with the chock-full-of-sausage gravy and stupendous

❶ Customers flocked back to Ward's Dairy Bar & Grill when Judy Ward reopened the diner in 2010. One reason is surely the late Charlie Ward's legendary sausage, tangy and tender and made right there at the restaurant. ❷ A hungry lunch crowd lines up for hot dogs.

chili. Business has been brisk, but Ward says what pleases her is spending time with all the regulars, some of whom have been coming to the grill since they were children: "I'm just so glad I could bring it back."

Windy City Grill
2514 North Center Street, Hickory
(828) 322-1131

Don't miss the sausage-egg-and-double-cheese-on-a-bun sandwich

Ellen Fountain remembers going to the Windy City Grill with her husband when they were freshmen at Lenoir-Rhyne College 20 years ago. "And 10 a.m. on Monday, Wednesday, and Friday were the times to go," she says. Never mind that Lenoir-Rhyne's convocations just happened to take place at 10 a.m. on Mondays, Wednesdays, and Fridays. Fountain insists she visited the grill then for the very same reason she goes now: "They have the best sausage-egg-and-double-cheese-on-a-bun sandwich."

Students still frequent the grill, which has an atmosphere Fountain describes as cozy. "It's not a place you have to get fixed up to go to," she says. "It caters to the blue-collar population, and most guys show up in their coveralls for breakfast." Now a seventh-grade teacher in Newton, which is only 10 minutes from Hickory, Fountain and her family still find their way to the Windy City Grill once a week. "We are raising our children on sausage-egg-and-double-cheese-on-a-bun breakfast sandwiches," she says. "And they're thriving."

The sausage-egg-and-double-cheese-on-a-bun sandwich at Windy City Grill is a tradition for some families.

Alfred & Charlie's BBQ House
815 South New Hope Road,
Gastonia (704) 864-4446

Don't miss the French toast

Robin Estes admits that it's unusual to find superb French toast in a barbecue restaurant. Estes was born in Statesville and now lives in Lake Wylie, South Carolina, 20 minutes from Alfred & Charlie's.

The food at Alfred & Charlie's, as you'd expect in a barbecue restaurant, is hearty fare — platters anchored by thick pork chops, big links of pork sausage, patties of livermush, or huge country ham steaks. And then there's the Gourmet BBQ Omelet. "You really need to be hungry for this item," says Estes. "I order it with just one egg and can't eat all of it. It's stuffed with pork barbecue, along with chopped grilled peppers, onions, salsa, and cheddar cheese." But be warned, Estes says: "It has a little bite to it with the salsa and a secret spice, but the combination of all the flavors explodes in your mouth."

Estes and her husband, Jeff, prefer the French toast. "The taste is still light, although it's soaked in milk and egg and fried in butter. I love the light coating of powdered sugar on top. It melts in your mouth." But the best part about eating Alfred & Charlie's French toast, Estes says, is the memories it brings back: "It just reminds me of my childhood and how my grandmother made French toast."

The French toast at Alfred and Charlie's BBQ House in Gastonia melts in your mouth - and takes you back to mornings at grandma's.

Knight's on Main
870 Main Street, Blowing Rock
(828) 295-3869

Don't miss the livermush

"When you find a place that will carry livermush or cook an egg to order, you hang on to it," says Tracy Brown, executive director of the Blowing Rock Tourism Development Authority. That place is Knight's on Main. "It's a local favorite that serves a good helping of comfort food with a strong dash of Southern hospitality."

And Neese's livermush. "Mr. and Mrs. Tom Neese have a home here," Brown says. The staff members have shirts that say "peace, love and livermush."

"It's a versatile thing, that livermush," says Brown, who's originally from Burlington.

"You can have it on a club biscuit; add some lettuce, tomatoes, pickles, and mayonnaise, and you've got a perfect breakfast that will fit in your hand."

PHOTOGRAPHY BY ©ISTOCKPHOTO.COM/SUBJUG

Books Toys Music & Crafts

HOTOGRAPHY BY ©ISTOCKPHOTO.COM/IDEABUG

Malaprop's

WHILE OVERCOMING THE LITERARY PERSECUTION OF HER CHILDHOOD, EMÖKE B'RACZ ESTABLISHED ASHEVILLE'S SIGNATURE BOOKSTORE.

By Janet Hurley

PHOTOGRAPHY BY MATT ROSE

Emöke B'Racz, 62, sits in the cafe of Malaprop's Bookstore, which she opened in downtown Asheville in 1982.

It's easy to understand, while browsing Malaprop's eclectic mix of titles — from the best sellers to the overlooked to the once-banned — that B'Racz has spent the past 29 years reclaiming books stolen from her family so long ago.

In the process, she created a literary hub for western North Carolina — a bookstore, she says, that's about creativity and community.

B'Racz opened Malaprop's — derived from "malapropism," meaning ludicrous misuse of a word — without business loans. She depended, instead, on common sense and honesty.

In 2000, Malaprop's received the Seal of the City Recognition for Outstanding Contributions to the City of Asheville, the same year Publishers Weekly named it Bookseller of the Year.

Today, Malaprop's customers, both locals and tourists, peruse titles in a space where the lighting is warm but not dim and the signage is hand-lettered. Authors smile down from colorful event posters lining the walls. And not just best-selling authors, although the store invites many. Malaprop's embraces emerging local and regional talents. "There are books — and writers — I need to be there for," B'Racz says.

For almost 30 years, Asheville residents have depended on Emöke B'Racz for their book-buying needs.

Visit

Malaprop's Bookstore
55 Haywood Street
Asheville, N.C. 28801
(828) 254-6734
malaprops.com

Don't Miss

Pick up a copy of *27 Views of Asheville,* a collection of essays, poetry, and short stories by some of western North Carolina's finest writers, including Ron Rash, Sharyn McCrumb, Gail Godwin, Charles Frazier, and Robert Morgan.

WORLD ALMANAC
2012
North Carolina CURIOSITIES
Farm Fresh
North Carolina
ROSENBERG
TEHRAN
DOGOPOLY

Highland Books

IN BREVARD, ONE COUPLE ENCOURAGES COMMUNITY MEMBERS TO EXPLORE THE WORLD AROUND THEM.

By Katie Baer

PHOTOGRAPHY BY MATT ROSE

Tim and Peggy Hansen saw Brevard as a beginning. They had a romantic notion of establishing a bookstore, making it a success, selling it, and then moving on to start another store farther up the Blue Ridge Parkway. They planned to repeat the pattern every few years.

But a funny thing happened on the way to their dream plan: They fell in love with Brevard and couldn't imagine moving on. So they committed themselves to building Highland Books, located just blocks from downtown, as a business and an anchor in the community.

Thirty-six years after the couple purchased the store in 1976, Tim and Peggy see Highland Books as an opportunity to educate Brevard residents about the area around them. They stock trail maps for the Pisgah National Forest, DuPont State Forest, and Panthertown; guides to North Carolina waterfalls; and the Trails Illustrated map for the national forests of western North Carolina.

The Hansens feel a zeal for promoting reading among all members of their community. They helped build a library for a local after-school tutoring program. They collaborate with the Transylvania County library when it holds lectures with nationally known authors. And they display the current book selections of the 18 local reading groups.

Tim and Peggy Hansen now have 35 years worth of roots in this small town in western North Carolina. And that's a beginning to be proud of.

❶ Tim and Peggy Hansen offer Brevard residents stacks of books by North Carolina authors. ❷ A customer browses all that Highland Books has to offer.

Visit

Highland Books
277 North Broad Street
Brevard, N.C. 28712
(828) 884-2424
Hours: Monday-Saturday, 9:30 a.m.-5:30 p.m.

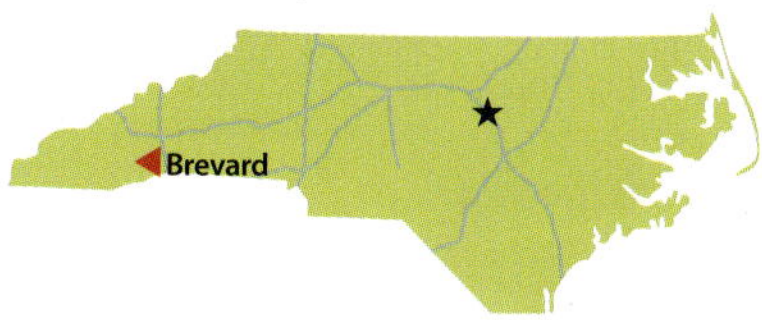

O.P. TAYLOR'S
The Coolest Toy Store On The Planet

1

2

UGLYDOLL
playmobil

3

O.P. Taylor's

IT'S ALL FUN AND GAMES FOR JOHN TAYLOR, FOUNDER AND OWNER OF A TOY STORE IN DOWNTOWN BREVARD.

By Heidi Coryell Williams

PHOTOGRAPHY BY WHITEBOX WEDDINGS

An air raid siren sounds, but no one flinches. Maybe it's the horn's volume, or lack of it, that fails to induce alarm. Or maybe it's because anything goes in this multilevel toy store in the heart of historic downtown Brevard. Here, reality is suspended, age is irrelevant, and a siren is simply a ringing cell phone.

John Taylor's 6,000-square-foot toy shop — a mainstay in Brevard since the late 1980s — is a tribute to his lifelong pursuit of happiness.

The interior is a maze of color and activity. Its contents range from the familiar — pink rain boots with lime-green butterflies, an orange magnifying glass, a long, draping, plush snake — to the slightly odd, such as ventriloquism gear. For every toy that stretches the imagination at O.P. Taylor's, it seems there are two more stocked purely to feed folks' habits. Model train habits. Slot car habits. Erector construction toy habits.

❶ On the outside, the building at the corner of South Broad and Main streets hasn't changed much in 70 years. The inside, however, is a different world. ❷ and ❸ Wyatt Owen and Erin Haile are as happy as kids in a ... well, toy store. And John Taylor is right there with them.

Almost everyone here finds his way to the Carnival, a small city of Lionel trains stretching roughly the length and width of several foosball tables. Green buttons control more than a dozen different mechanical scenes, at the center of which stands a Ferris wheel, elaborately constructed beneath a Plexiglas roof.

This is the South's toy store. A little eccentric, a lot of fun. Tread freely.

Go Play

O.P. Taylor's
2 South Broad Street
Brevard, N.C. 28712
(800) 500-TOYS (8697)
optaylors.com

Don't Miss

Brevard is home to an unusually large population of white squirrels, which the township celebrates with everything from an annual music festival to a squirrel box derby.

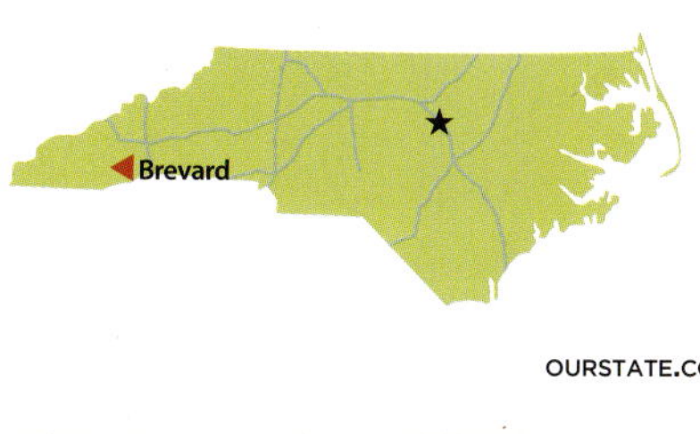

Jens Kruger

The Kruger Brothers

AMERICAN MUSIC INSPIRED TWO BROTHERS IN EUROPE TO PICK UP THEIR GUITARS AND BANJOS, AND SEEK OUT THE SOUND OF APPALACHIA.

By David Menconi

PHOTOGRAPHY BY CHERYL ZIBISKY

When Jens Kruger tunes up his banjo, you hear echoes of different European influences — French, Irish, Italian, and his native German — and flourishes that make the instrument sound like flamenco guitar or even Indian sitar. And he's not afraid to bend notes to turn them blue.

"Maybe you'll hear a little bit of where your ancestors come from in this next piece," Jens says from his seat on the stage of Raleigh's Fletcher Opera Theater with his brother, Uwe, beside him.

That's his introduction for Appalachian Concerto, the Kruger Brothers' most full-flowered expression of Jens's diverse musical style. The Kruger Brothers released *Appalachian Concerto* in 2011, and it's evocative enough to make you feel like you've wandered into Doc Watson's hometown of Deep Gap with a string quartet in tow.

The Krugers moved from Switzerland to Wilkesboro in 2003. But their history with American music began when they listened to country radio as children. Jens and Uwe started playing the guitar and banjo, and Jens came to America in the early 1980s to play with the patron saint of bluegrass, Bill Monroe.

In 1995, Jens and Uwe connected with Landsberg to form the Kruger Brothers. With an ensemble approach more like a classical string quartet than a bluegrass band, they forged an elegant musical blend steeped in European and American styles.

.eft to right: Jens Kruger, Uwe Kruger, ınd Joel Landsberg make up the Kruger 3rothers trio.

Listen

To purchase CDs and check upcoming show dates, visit krugerbrothers.com.

The must-listen album is the Kruger Brother's *Appalachian Concerto*, commissioned by the Ashe County Arts Council with songs that evoke aspects of beauty, wildness, and scale from the viewpoint of a new arrival.

DOGWOOD
CRAFTERS
A CRAFT COOPERATIVE

Dogwood Crafters

MAKING CRAFTS IN DILLSBORO HELPS HEAL THE PEOPLE WHO MAKE THE COMMUNITY.

By Michael Graff

PHOTOGRAPHY BY EMILY CHAPLIN & CHRIS COUNCIL

After Brenda Anders' father died n 1984, a friend gave her a box of npainted ceramic figurines.

"You need therapy," her friend said.

Anders took the box into the asement of her home up a crooked oad on the side of a mountain just utside of Dillsboro, and she decorated or weeks, just her and her hands and ome work.

Busy hands and busy minds can be ound in just about every basement nd workshop spread among the trees nd hills around Dillsboro. When hese mountain people lose a piece of hemselves, when they have time to ill, they create something. Dillsboro, tiny town with a dozen or so shops n a couple or so streets an hour or so vest of anywhere, is draped in arts and crafts, and it's threaded together by inspiration of all kinds.

That inspiration — plucked from places high on the Great Smoky Mountains and down on the Tuckasegee River and from memories that go back to Grandma and her first knitting lesson — comes together in a material form at a place called Dogwood Crafters Co-op.

Dogwood Crafters is a place, made up of a group of old log cabins renovated and put together on the corner of town closest to the river. All of the items in the shop are handmade and for sale.

Dogwood Crafters is also an organization, made up of about 100 artists and crafters who pay commission to be a part of the group. They are old and young; some are full-time artists and some are just doing it for fun. And others are doing it because they can't imagine a life without it.

'he log-cabin exterior of Dogwood :rafters fits the mountain scenery of)illsboro, and the crafts found inside it the personalities of the people who nake them.

1

2

3

The place smells ike a candlelit ountry home. t's inviting, and ustomers come ack year after year.

The commitment to using only andmade products is the foundation f the co-op, which started in 1976 nside a home on Church Street. The rafters sold $158 worth of items on he first day. Now, they're regularly clipsing $300,000 a year in sales.

The model for the co-op is simple, ut it's helped Dogwood Crafters ecome one of the most successful raft co-ops in the country. Everything s done by volunteers. A craftsperson vho works in the shop pays only 20 ercent commission to Dogwood Crafters. One who doesn't help work ays 40 percent. They help each other.

The place smells like a candlelit ountry home. It's inviting, and ustomers come back year after year.

On the other side of every item is crafter.

❶ Whether she's baking cookies for the group or visiting someone in the hospital, Brenda Anders finds plenty of ways to take care of her fellow members of Dogwood Crafters. ❷ and ❸ The items inside Dogwood Crafters vary: from the decorative, such as the flower boutonnieres, to the quirky, such as a birdhouse made from a cowboy boot.

Linda Parrish retired here after a career as a schoolteacher in Georgia. She makes cards, notepads, and stamp art, and she's the president of the Dillsboro Crafters.

Patricia Cowan is from the area, and she was one of the 12 people who answered the advertisement in *The Sylva Herald*. She paints.

Barbara Wehler lived in Asheville, a town known for its arts, but she and her husband moved to Sylva just to be closer to Dogwood Crafters.

There's a reason the crafters are drawn to these hills; they're drawn to each other.

Madge Fala carves and paints gourds. A year ago, her son died. When she was at the hospital, she looked up, and several of the crafters had come to support her.

Shirley Cox's husband has been sick for years, and doctors continue to say he might not make it much longer. When she can, Cox sews. She makes dolls; the Dogwood family won't let her stop.

"She needs Dogwood," Anders says. "We all do."

Visit

Dogwood Crafters
90 Webster Street
Dillsboro, N.C. 28725
(828) 586-2248

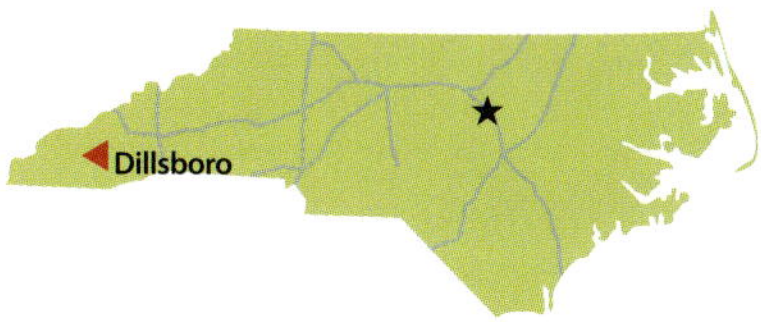

STAY

PHOTOGRAPHY BY ©ISTOCKPHOTO.COM/IPIDJOE

Chalet Inn

FOR 18 YEARS, AN INN ON A MOUNTAIN BETWEEN DILLSBORO AND BRYSON CITY HAS BEEN THE HOME OF GEORGE AND HANNEKE WARE.

By Jeremy Markovich

PHOTOGRAPHY BY EMILY CHAPLIN & CHRIS COUNCIL

George and Hanneke Ware bought the land for the Chalet Inn 21 years ago from a real estate agent who didn't think to show it to them because it wasn't worth much. Back then, it was just a neglected farmhouse surrounded by a sheath of brush and a tangle of weeds and vines in the middle of 22 forested acres. It took five years of searching, from Pickens, South Carolina, to Gatlinburg, Tennessee, from Boone to Robbinsville, to find this place. It was perfect.

The land is rugged and deep and still hard for humans to tame.

The Wares transformed a neglected farmhouse into a secluded escape in the woods of western North Carolina.

Here is Jackson County, a place that sits west of 98 percent of North Carolina's population. Just down the road, right next to each other, are Dillsboro and then Sylva, with quiet, nostalgic streets and cute restaurants along the Tuckasegee River. Go a little farther, and you can take a ride on a historic steam locomotive. Or you can shoot craps at Harrah's. It's all within a 12-minute drive.

But what you cannot escape from, the things that are everywhere and surround you and are always in your consciousness, are the mountains. They loom over you wherever you go, casting shadows and wrapping themselves around you. The land is rugged and deep and still hard for humans to tame.

1

2

MiddleValley
ToSquirrel Ridge
To Tired Mans Escape
To Mountain Laurel
3

It took three years of sweat and dirty hands and sawdust to get the place open.

It was this land that drew in George, and the area turned out to be perfect. The hardwoods of western North Carolina remind Hanneke of the Black Forest in Germany. A Bavarian home was meant to be here. While in Germany, George fell in love with gasthauses — little country inns so small that you had no choice but to bump into the owners and talk and eat and learn. George wanted one of his own. He wanted a big mountain home but couldn't afford it unless he opened it for guests.

In August 1990, they bought the land and started pulling weeds and calling in carpenters and craftsmen to build a new gasthaus up in their new cove. It took three years of sweat and dirty hands and sawdust to get the place open. They built balconies and rerouted the stream. They planted grass and put in a pond.

❶ George Ware met his wife, Hanneke, in the Netherlands, fell in love, and brought her and a little bit of Europe to western North Carolina. ❷ Reminders of Hanneke's Dutch roots decorate the inn. ❸ Signs direct guests to relaxing spots on the inn's property.

They stocked the library with books, made some of George's old military relics into plaques, and hung them on the walls. Even after guests started arriving, the work wasn't finished. Money trickled in, and once enough of it arrived, George and Hanneke gutted the rooms and redid them.

A while back, they had a decision to make. They were booked solid; on July and October weekends they were turning away three times as many people as they had rooms. They were working seven days a week. They could either sell this place and move on, or expand and hire more staff.

They built a new set of rooms in a new building at the top of a hill. From up there, you can see the pond, the fountain, the fire pit, and the stream. You can see Double Top Mountain and the Blue Ridge. You can see it all. And you look down at the Chalet Inn and see what George and Hanneke see.

Home.

Visit

Chalet Inn
285 Lone Oak Drive
Dillsboro, N.C. 28725
(828) 586-0251
chaletinn.com

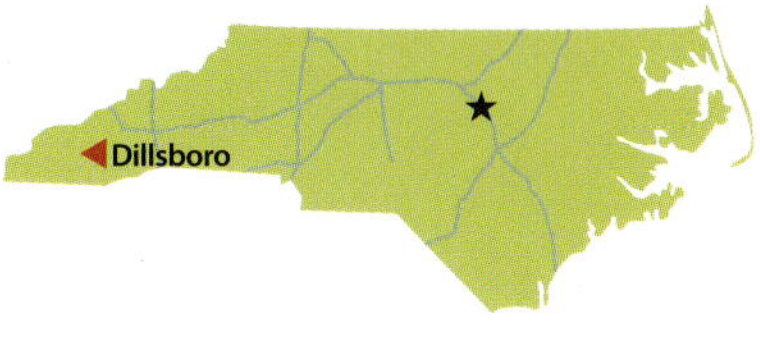

Boyd Mountain Cabins

ON THEIR SMALL MOUNTAIN IN HAYWOOD COUNTY, DAN AND BETSY BOYD PUT SPECIAL CARE INTO EVERY PIECE OF WOOD.

By Jeri Rowe

PHOTOGRAPHY BY MATT ROSE

Dan and Betsy Boyd collect log cabins. Dan climbs into his pickup and prowls the back roads for days. He looks for cabins in the bend of a curve, in the middle of a field, or back through the woods where nobody has lived for years.

Dan and Betsy have saved at least a dozen cabins. They've moved the buildings to their small mountain near the Great Smoky Mountains National Park. On Boyd Mountain, in Haywood County, Dan and Betsy have restored these log cabins to a splendor never seen during the cabins' previous lives, which extend back at least 150 years. Inside the two-story cabins, which the Boyds rent out to visitors, you'll see their handiwork, such as fireplaces of stacked stone, cabinets painted green, and antique kitchen tables. There are also conveniences of a 21st-

One of the Boyds' cabins sits in the middle of their tree farm on the mountain they own.

He heard about the history of these logs, of where they came from and the people they housed.

century life: Each cabin has a stove, a refrigerator, wireless Internet, a washer, a dryer, and a wide-screen TV. And always on the first floor, in a frame, you'll find the cabins' history.

In third grade, Dan wrote that he wanted to be a dentist and live in a log cabin. He'd seen his uncle Ben restore log cabins and turn them into a vacation spot called Pioneer Village in Maggie Valley. He heard about the history of these logs, of where they came from and the people they housed. So, after Mars Hill College and dental school in Virginia, Dan bought the family farm created by his paternal grandfather on Boyd Mountain.

In 1967, he met Betsy Robertson on a blind date. Three years later, they were married. In the early 1970s, they bought 130 acres on Boyd Mountain. Dan rebuilt a log cabin he discovered in nearby Madison County while Betsy planted azaleas.

The cabin was small — 400 square feet — when they moved into it in the spring of 1974. But Dan saw it as home. He and Betsy raised two children, David and Mary Alice, inside their log cabin, and over the years, Dan discovered three other log cabins to create a bigger home for his family. In the process, he and Betsy resurrected the Boyd family farm.

By 1988, Dan and Betsy had completed their log cabin home, creating a 4,000-square-foot showplace, full of antiques.

Dan never could shake his log cabin fever. So, in 1989, he started finding them, fixing them, and turning them into rentals for vacationers. He bought a log cabin every two years or so. These days, Dan still climbs into his pickup and drives the back roads to look for logs that speak to him.

Dan and Betsy Boyd restore and rebuild cabins for vacationers looking for a rustic mountain getaway.

Visit

Boyd Mountain Log Cabins
445 Boyd Farm Road
Waynesville, N.C. 28785
(828) 926-1575
boydmountain.com

Don't Miss

Pick up one of the walking sticks the Boyds keep in each cabin, and hike one of the trails that fork from the property. Or fish for trout in one of the three stocked ponds.

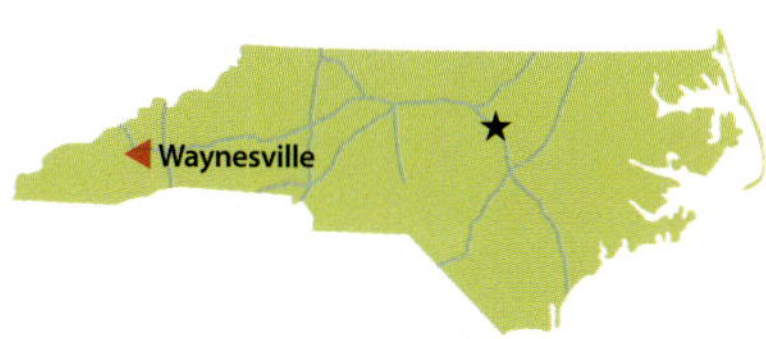